FULFILLING
THE VISION

FULFILLING THE VISION

Collaborative Ministry in the Parish

HOWARD J. HUBBARD

A Crossroad Herder Book
The Crossroad Publishing Company
New York

Fulfilling the Vision was first presented at the National Conference for Pastoral Planning and Council Development in Seattle, Wash., on March 10, 1996. The transcript of the presentation has been edited for publication.

The Crossroad Publishing Company
370 Lexington Avenue, New York, NY 10017

Printed in the United States of America

Cataloging-in-Publication data is available from the Library of Congress, Washington, D.C.

Library of Congress Catalog Card No.: 98-70962
ISBN 0-8245-1719-9

1 2 3 4 5 6 7 8 9 10   02 01 00 99 98

For the vision still has its time,
presses on to fulfillment,
and will not disappoint;
if it delays wait for it,
it will surely come,
it will not be late.

— Habakkuk 2:3

Contents

Contents

• 8 •

Preface

I WOULD LIKE to seize this opportunity to express my deep gratitude and appreciation and that of my brother bishops for the extraordinary contribution all those involved with pastoral planning and council development have made and continue to make to the church in the United States.

They have truly been pioneers, exploring new pathways, opening up new frontiers with few if any guidelines, blueprints, or road maps to follow. By and large it has been a method of trial and error, seeking to bring the disciplines of planning, group dynamics, and organizational development to bear upon the rapidly changing ecclesiological, theological, and sociological scene in contemporary American Catholicism.

They have been learning by doing and by sharing with one another in the field the fruits of their own professional and personal experiences, both positive and negative. And in so doing they have rendered an invaluable service to God's people even though at times their best efforts have been taken for granted, ignored, ridiculed, criticized, or rejected outright.

So I thank them profusely for their dedication and commitment, for their patience and perseverance, for their vision and sense of the church, for their ingenuity, creativity, sensitivity, and flexibility, and for their sterling witness to how the concepts of collegiality, collaboration, and shared responsibility are lived in practice.

They are truly instruments of hope in an age of uncertainty and despair, beacons of light in a time of darkness and turmoil, agents of change in an era of chaos and confusion, and heralds of the good news in a church, world, and society that so desperately need good news.

I also want to acknowledge the enormous contributions of Father Michael Farano, Joe Powers, John Chupka, and Sister Kathleen Turley, who have staffed our office of pastoral planning over the past twenty-four years, without whose support, dedication, and commitment I would have little to say on the topic at hand. I also wish to acknowledge the wisdom and insights I have garnered from my interaction with the Conference for Pastoral Planning and Council Development over the past twenty-three years, and in particular from the marvelous study on parish restructuring conducted by Joe Verla and John Flaherty (*Diocesan Efforts at Parish Reorganization,* published by the Conference for Pastoral Planning and Council Development, 1995).

FULFILLING
THE VISION

Chapter 1

A Shared Vision

HERE I WILL offer some theological reflections on parish restructuring. Let
me begin by issuing some disclaimers. First,
I make no pretense to be a theologian. Second, I realize that many have as much or
greater experience in the whole area of parish restructuring and thus are as qualified or
indeed more qualified than I to offer these
reflections. Third, I have no illusions about
breaking new ground. Rather I would simply like to offer some personal reflections and
observations based upon my experience in
the diocese of Albany:

- in conducting a formal visitation program to all
  196 of the parishes in our diocese,

- in being involved in the closure, merger, or consolidation of some twenty parish communities,

- in formulating, as a result of a diocesan-wide consultation, criteria for vital and viable parish communities,

- and in undertaking a two-year diocesan-wide planning process to provide comprehensive pastoral services to our people in light of contemporary realities.

Therefore, I offer these reflections, not as a final word or even as a draft working paper but simply with the hope that this sharing based upon the experience of our local church will serve to prime the pump for fertile reflections and discussion on this topic that is of such critical importance for the church in the United States.

I saw recently a video by Joel Barker, a futurologist, that offers a cogent presentation on the power of vision to create a sense of hope, purpose, and meaning, to develop an esprit de corps, and especially to carry people through periods of turbulence and change such as we have been experiencing and will continue to experience in the life of the church.

In his presentation, Barker states that there are four key ingredients for a vision community:

1. The vision needs to be developed by leaders (not created by the masses). Leaders, of course, must listen to their people, but they must take the input received and fashion it into a coherent, powerful vision.

2. The vision of the leader must be shared with the team, and the team must agree to own and support it. There must, in other words, be agreement or consensus on the direction.

3. The vision must be comprehensive and detailed. Generalities just won't do. All must know how they are going to participate and to contribute.

4. The vision must be positive and inspiring. It must be worth the effort and investment made to achieve it.

All of us within the church — bishops, priests, deacons, religious, and laity — need to be in conversation or dialogue with one another about the vision. This cannot be stressed strongly enough because so often the disagreements or obstacles that arise in pastoral planning and parish restructuring stem from the fact that people are operating with different ecclesiologies or different models of the church and do not share the same view. We can't live and act, therefore, with the quiet assumption that we are all at the same place. We need to talk things out theologically and ecclesiologically.

And this is especially true when we talk about parish restructuring. For change is never easy, and it becomes particularly traumatic when it affects one's faith community. There are so many cherished memories and deep emotional feelings associated with the place people have gathered for weekly worship, have celebrated the rites of passage, have attended school or received religious instruction or socialized together over the years.

In other words when people have formed closely knit communities based upon language, ethnic customs, or neighborhood ties, it is most painful to think about changes in worship sites, staffing patterns, or ways of rendering and receiving pastoral services. Any change, therefore, must be approached with the utmost sensitivity and with a view to preserving as far as possible natural communities and established customs and traditions.

However, all of this must be done within the framework of what is practically feasible, fiscally possible, and pastorally reasonable. It can be accomplished, in other words, only by shedding narrow parochialisms and being receptive to the ministry of others besides the traditional pastoral caregiver in the church.

I would like to offer a vision for parish restructuring that will help all in the church, clergy, religious, and laity, to face the challenges that confront us not so much as problems to be solved but as opportunities to develop new models and approaches to parish life and ministry that are truly creative, innovative, and future-oriented.

Chapter 2

Foundations
for the Vision

T HE FIRST ASSUMPTION is that the concept of shared responsibility and collaborative ministry, based upon the baptismal call that is given to each member of the church, must serve as a foundation for the church's efforts to advance the mission and ministry of Jesus in our world.

In other words, while there can be many reasons why a diocese might engage in parish restructuring, for example, the priest shortage, shifting demographics, or economics, from my perspective the primary reason to engage in parish restructuring is the baptismal call and its implications for the ministry that belongs to every Christian. Therefore, even if there were a superabundance of ordained clergy and ample fiscal resources to implement the parish's mission, there would still be the need to engage in parish restructuring based upon a better appreciation of the theology of baptism and collaborative ministry.

The second assumption underlying this vision is that the parish community has been and will continue to be the center of the church's life. Our diocesan efforts must be geared to strengthening and to supporting people at the parochial level in the fourfold ministry of the church: in proclaiming the Gospel, in worshiping, in building community, and in offering healing services to people in need.

Before considering these themes of shared responsibility and the centrality of the parish for Catholic Christian life, however, it is necessary to reflect first upon the church itself, because our vision of the church and its mission influences our understanding of ministry and shapes its development in the parish community.

The Church as Living Mystery

When we speak of the church, we are dealing with a living mystery. As the Second Vatican Council expressed it, "The church is a mystery prefigured in creation, prepared in the history of Israel, initiated by the Holy Spirit, and reaching its fulfillment only at the end of time" (*Dogmatic Constitution on the Church*, par. 2). The church is that mystery in which God's saving presence is made visible in Christ Jesus.

Because the church is a mystery, therefore, it cannot be totally understood or fully defined. But, from its very beginning, the church has been revealed to be a community of people formed by the word of God, animated by the creative power of the Holy Spirit, and sustained by the worship and service of its

members. Its mission is both to proclaim the
message of Christ for the enlightenment of
the hearts and minds of people, and to provide a place where his healing presence can be
experienced. As such, the church must always
understand itself as not existing for itself but
for the world. The church can never be a mission or ministry unto itself; rather, it is to be a
community of ministers charged with the task
of bringing the healing presence of Christ to
a wounded humanity.

We who belong to the church today, then,
are called to be the community described in
the New Testament, where all things were
held in common, where Paul urged that competition should be in giving service, and
where Jesus said that those who would be
great should be the servants of all people.

Shared Responsibility

The Second Vatican Council has given us a
concept that enables us to be the church,

the community of God's people in our day: the concept of shared responsibility. Put succinctly, shared responsibility means that each of us, by virtue of baptism, has the right and the duty to participate in Christ's mission of praising and worshiping the Lord, of teaching God's word, of serving God's people, and of building a community here on earth in preparation for the fullness of life together in the kingdom of heaven.

Through baptism, in other words, every Christian is brought into an intimate, personal, and abiding union with Jesus and with all other Christians. This sacramental dignity unites popes, bishops, priests, deacons, religious, and laity in the one Body of Christ, which is the church. It also serves as a mandate to each of us to use our talents so that the mission of Christ and his church may be fulfilled.

This responsibility of being about the work of Christ's church is ours, regardless of our state in life or the differing roles we may actually exercise. We are all called to be co-creators with God, advancing the Lord's kingdom in our day. Every person's contribution is vitally needed so that, together in a rich diversity, we can build up the Christian community by enhancing the sacredness and growth of others.

Shared responsibility, then, is neither a luxury nor a concession. Rather, it is a necessary and perennial dimension of the life of the church, exercised by those who are rooted in the living and loving relationship with Christ. It demands interdependence and partnership between bishops and priests, between clergy, religious, and laity, and between parish and diocese.

Before any distinction of roles or offices in the church, in other words, we stand as one family of the baptized. It is the exercise of the collective priesthood of the baptized that most fully continues the sacramental presence of Christ in the world.

While the concept of shared responsibility appreciates the distinction between the common priesthood of the faithful and the ministerial or hierarchical priesthood, which is rooted in the apostolic succession and vested in the power and responsibility of the ordained to act in the person of Christ, it also recognizes that these modes of participation in the priesthood of Christ are ordered to one another so that the ministerial priesthood is at the service of the common priesthood and directed to the unfolding of the baptismal grace of all Christians. (*Catechism of the Catholic Church*, 1547)

Hence, the concept of shared responsibility emphasizes that the church is not a stratified or clerically dominated society but a community of persons, all sharing in the priesthood of Jesus Christ and all called equally to be the people of God.

It stresses, furthermore, that the church is a community of collaborative ministry, that is, a community in which each member is challenged to see his or her baptism as a call to holiness and ministry, a community that seeks to help its members discern the personal charisms given them by the Spirit and to enable them to employ their gifts in the mission of the church, a community whose

ordained and vowed ministers see the fostering of greater participation in the work of the
church as essential to their responsibility as
leaders.

If we truly believe with the Second Vatican Council, then, that the church exists to
carry out the priestly ministry of Jesus, and
if we believe with the council that the laity
are joined with bishops, priests, deacons, and
vowed religious as enactors of that mission,
then what we have is a church of ministers: some of them bishops, some of them
priests, some of them deacons, some of them
vowed religious, but most of them lay men
and women. Such an understanding of the
church allows for the richness of varied ministerial roles and encourages all the members
of the church to contribute the wonderful
gifts each has.

This vision of a universally ministering
church can be summarized as follows: responsibility for the mission of the church is
collaborative and is shared by all the baptized — ordained and nonordained; vowed

and nonvowed; carpenter, housewife, business executive; young and old; rich and poor; parent, child, single person; black, white, red, yellow, and brown — all bound together by a variety of gifts and ministries and all serving the one priestly mission of our Lord Jesus Christ.

Faith Lived in Community

This brings me to my second major assumption, namely, that the parish community is where people receive the education, formation, support, and spiritual nourishment they need to fulfill this call to shared responsibility, this call to exercise the priestly ministry of Jesus in our world today.

One of the distinctive notes of the Christian life is its communal character, that is, Jesus Christ called his followers to faith, but faith lived in community. The church he founded was to be a living community of persons, not an aggregate of individual believers.

Thus, from the very beginning of Christian history those who responded to Christ's call to discipleship gathered themselves together into a community formed by the word of God, animated by the creative power of the Holy Spirit, and sustained by the worship and service of its members.

The Acts of the Apostles, that book of sacred scripture which recounts the development of the church following the death and resurrection of Jesus, describes how early Christians shared their beliefs, experiences, values, and ideals by forming worship communities of word and sacrament: "They devoted themselves to the apostles' instructions and communal life, to the breaking of the bread and prayers" (Acts 2:42).

The fruit of this faith sharing was service to others: "None of the members was ever in want, as all those who owned land or houses would sell them and bring money from them to present to the apostles; it was then distributed to any members who might be in need" (Acts 4:34–35).

Down through the course of history the followers of Jesus have struggled to preserve or to keep alive that sense of community, that spirit of worship, love, and service that existed in the apostolic church.

While this effort has expressed itself in a variety of forms in diverse historical, social, and cultural settings, that vehicle for fostering Christian life and growth which has survived to the present time and which has proven most effective as the spiritual descendant of the early Christian community is that stable gathering of persons known as the parish.

The parish, then, is meant to be a group of Christians who pray and worship together and who extend that worship into their everyday lives by helping each other with spiritual, emotional, and financial support.

Hearing this, some may say, "That's what a parish is supposed to be? That's not my experience of parish. I don't find a sense of community in my parish. Oh, it's a place where I go for weekend Mass or to receive the sacraments, but not to experience community, not to gain a sense of belonging or acceptance. It's too large and impersonal; it's only concerned with one aspect of my life, my spiritual needs, but with little, if any, attention paid to my daily struggles as a parent, worker, student, or person just trying to make it in a swirl of personal, social, and economic problems."

It is true that many parishes are not the caring Christian communities they are meant to be. Problems of size or finances, of apathetic membership or indifferent leadership have prevented some parishes from becoming the alive, dynamic, vibrant centers of Christian faith and service they are designed to be.

Thus many look elsewhere to find community: to spiritual groups that function largely outside parish structures, groups like Marriage Encounter, Charismatic Renewal, the Cursillo Movement, or to support groups for the separated and divorced, widows and

widowers, or to social clubs and neighborhood organizations, to fraternal organizations or hobby groups, or even to bars and
taverns. Yes, sad to say, bars and taverns
offer to some a greater sense of community
than many find in their parish. Still there are
others who are bereft of a sense of community altogether. They live lonely isolated
lives of quiet desperation in an increasingly
dehumanized and depersonalized world and
society.

Chapter 3

The Parish Today

S OME TODAY gloomily predict the demise of the parish or suggest that the parish structure has become obsolete or irrelevant to the needs of today.

Quite frankly, I hold quite the opposite assumption, namely, that while the parish has problems, its structure is more needed today than ever before and it will remain as a hub or center of the church's life.

I stress the need for the parish today and in the future because with the growing number of forces undermining the stability of family life and with the increasing mobility of our society with its concomitant fruits of isolation, alienation, and depersonalization, there is less structure in our nation for people to come together and to support each other through mutual interdependence. Yet the basis of our Christian faith and indeed of healthy human living depends upon this mutual interdependence, upon our willingness to be aware of and concerned about one another. The parish is the place where this interdependence can and should happen, the place where support systems for Christian living and Christian service must constantly be developed and fashioned in light of changing needs and changing circumstances.

The Focus of the Parish

This does not suggest, of course, that all parish communities must function in the same way, or that the style of parish life in the future must be predicated on the past. Indeed forms of parish life must change and be ever responsive to the changing communities and people they serve.

There will always be need, however, for tangible structures whereby people can experience the loving presence of the Lord and build genuine community by sharing God's redemptive and liberating love with others. That structure is the parish community.

And the ultimate purpose of the structure we call the parish is to bring people into contact with Jesus Christ and the good news he proclaimed and to enable people to witness to common faith, love, and worship which the parish members share in communion with Jesus and one another.

Jesus, therefore, must be the focus of the parish's life. It is his mission that the parish must be about, his message that it must strive to communicate to others, his ministry that his members must seek to extend into the world. If this is not the case, if the Jesus dimension is not the central thread interwoven throughout all of the parish's life and activities and the ultimate norm and criterion by which its decisions are made and against which its results are evaluated, then the parish is little different in scope and purpose than that of a neighborhood association or fraternal organization. And its efforts, well motivated and well intentioned as they may be, and successful as they may be from a humanitarian or fiscal perspective, will fail to impart the life-giving power, strength, and inner peace that Jesus alone can give and for which people today are desperately hungry and thirsty.

Characteristics of a Vibrant Parish

Reflecting upon those parishes that are most vibrant and most successful, I believe there are certain ingredients common to them all, be they large or small parishes; in low-, moderate-, or high-income communities; or in urban, suburban, or rural settings. They are, in fact, the very characteristics identified by the National Conference of Catholic Bishops parish project as contributing to healthy, mature, spiritually alive parish communities. These characteristics are four in number.

1. Parishioners enjoy good liturgy and preaching. People earnestly desire worship services that help them to pray well and preaching that gives meaning to their faith lives. The Sunday Eucharist is an excellent opportunity for adult faith formation where the Scriptures are broken open and applied to daily life. At no other time do so many parishioners come together "as church" in one place. The parish expresses its identity at Sunday Eucharist and is sent forth to participate in the mission of Jesus. Our communal prayer ritualizes what we believe and how we live out our beliefs.

2. They value the ability of the parish to help people deal practically with their life concerns, such as alcohol and drug abuse, poor schools, crime and safety issues, unemployment, job instability, and especially their concerns about family and children. Parish support and small faith-sharing groups provide an arena where people can feel safe and understood, cared for and accepted. Parish ministries such as parish social outreach address the human concerns and also provide advocacy for the underserved. In this environment parish gatherings promote networking and peer ministry.

3. Parishioners need a feeling of ownership, a feeling that they belong, that their concerns are being

listened to and that they can have the opportunity to affect parish policy and practice. Parish leadership, including parish staff, parish pastoral council, and parish ministers can facilitate the creation of an environment which empowers parishioners to discover, develop, and utilize their gifts and talents in a way that gives them a sense of belonging and of contributing to the parish community.

4. The people appreciate an active quality in the parish, a sense that something is going on and that there is something happening for everyone. Certainly, today with our computer technology, we have an opportunity to communicate more quickly and more effectively with our people so that they are aware of what is happening in their parish. Effective and updated parish bulletin boards and quality weekly bulletins are vehicles to inform parishioners of activities occurring at parish, cluster, deanery, and diocesan levels.

I propose that these four characteristics be the realistic goals toward which parishes should strive in order to facilitate and enable further growth and vitality in their respective faith communities and in any restructuring that takes place.

On the basis of my own experience and reflections as well as the conclusions of the parish reorganization study (see above p. 11), I would suggest that there are two seemingly contradictory trends in parish life today that, I think, must be balanced and harmonized.

Smaller Communities and Larger Clusters

The first is the trend toward smaller, more intimate faith communities within larger parish entities, à la the *comunidades de base,* the small Christian communities flourishing in Latin America, but geared to our cultural and social realities. People today are feeling very isolated and alienated in our increasingly dehumanized and depersonalized society and are searching for communities where they can share faith, hopes, expectations, and struggles and be nourished by communal prayer and reflection upon the scriptures. Therefore more and more we must find ways to divide parish communities that suffer from overgrowth into smaller units where a sense of community can be nurtured and fostered. For I am convinced that it's not poverty of goods or poverty of riches that is at the heart of our societal problems, but rather it's that people at all socioeconomic levels have lost a sense of their dignity and worth as human beings.

Thus, we could have perfect programs in model communities, put everyone on a guaranteed annual income, offer well-developed educational, social, and liturgical services in our parishes and still not get to the heart of what ails modern man or modern woman. It is only when we give testimony to what a person means and to what love means that we do something that is truly significant.

We must develop communities, then, that witness to the fact that we are concerned about persons and personal values, and the signs of that concern will be acts of warmth, kindness, and presence among the members. The more evident this affirming, community-building ministry becomes within our parishes, then the more credible and attractive our ministry of word and sacrament will be.

However, simultaneous with this need to foster smaller communities within our parishes in order to give people a sense of identity and belonging, there is a corresponding need for clustering of parishes in given geographic areas to break down the excessive parochialism that has too often stifled cooperation and our need for interdependence, and to mobilize the resources, both personal and fiscal, needed to accomplish the mission of the parish.

While large parish communities often have the resources to fulfill their own needs, many middle-sized and smaller parishes can most effectively fulfill their mission only by working in concert with neighboring parish communities or working on an ecumenical or interfaith basis. For example, very often parishes do not have the resources themselves to support a youth ministry program or quality adult education program, but pooling their resources with one or two neighboring parishes would provide the trained personnel and the numbers of participants to make these programs vibrant and worthwhile.

In addition, parish programs like the Rite of Christian Initiation for Adults, marriage preparation, and the operation of food pantries can often best be staffed and resourced on an interparochial basis, rather than each parish undertaking its own efforts with inadequate personnel or too few participants for the programs to be effective.

Already the planning process in our diocese has led to some wonderful examples of parishes banding together on a cluster basis, learning from each other, opening new horizons and possibilities, and generating a renewed sense of energy and enthusiasm on the part of staff and parishioners.

Strategic Priorities

If the assumptions for pastoral planning I have articulated, namely, that the life of the church is most meaningfully experienced in the parish and that the way to build or develop the parish is a commitment to collaborative ministry, then to make this vision of our parishes as communities of collaborative ministers a reality, I would suggest two strategic priorities.

The first of these priorities is rooted in the recognition that *collaborative ministry is not something that just happens. It must be articulated clearly so that everyone understands the vision;* it must be prepared for carefully, so that people, especially in leadership, have the skills to function in such a model; and, therefore, it must be nurtured and implemented patiently and sensitively.

Our ordained ministers and other parish staff, lay and religious, are the key for promoting this vision and its implementation at the local level. If they are to do this well, however, they not only must understand the theology of collaborative ministry but also must learn the skills of ministering themselves in a collaborative fashion and of enabling others to do so. If the parish leadership does not function in a collaborative fashion, in other words, it is most unlikely that the wider parish community will gain this facility.

For the vision of collaborative ministry to be realized, we need to provide those desiring to minister with the education and formation resources they require to serve well. This will necessitate the development of a broad continuum of educational and formational opportunities for our people.

To minister effectively, some, for example, will need to earn a professional degree at the undergraduate or graduate level in theology, sacred scripture, religious education, pastoral counseling, or other related disciplines. Some, to exercise their desired ministry, will need to take required courses that will enable them to be licensed or credentialed by some appropriate diocesan body. Some will need to take workshops or mini-courses to acquire the appropriate theological knowledge and pastoral skills for fulfilling their ministry.

All will need access to ongoing theological and pastoral education appropriate to their background, experience, and ministerial responsibilities. All will need retreat and other formational opportunities that will enable them to grow spiritually.

My point is this: to achieve the vision of collaborative ministry will require the availability of a variety of formal and informal educational and formational programs. Presently, some of these opportunities are available in a piecemeal fashion; others are simply nonexistent. If pastoral planning and parish restructuring are to flourish, then, a comprehensive network of programs must be put into place within our dioceses. And not only must there be programs for initial formation but for ongoing education as well. For if the pastoral planning process and its eventual implementation are to be a success, then all ministers within the church must continually be open to ongoing education and formation, making time for reading, listening to tapes, and attending workshops and lectures that will give the knowledge and skills needed to keep abreast of what's happening in scripture, theology, liturgy, and contemporary pastoral practice. And in keeping abreast, we must develop a balanced understanding of contemporary theological and pastoral issues, one that is fully in accord with the mind and heart of the church, and not just following the pet theories of our favorite guru or latching on to the fads of the moment.

Recently, Cardinal Godfried Danneels of Brussels indicated that the intellectual dimension of the church's life is more important today than ever before in history. The cardinal states that the challenge of our era is to create a dialogue between faith and science, religion and culture. But this can happen only if our efforts at evangelization have a sound philosophical basis, only if our catechesis has a strong cognitive content, and only if apologetics once again becomes part and parcel of the life of the church.

However, we can do this only to the extent that we are open to ongoing education and formation and are willing to discuss with each other ecclesiological and theological issues. And if we are not willing to do this, then we will stunt our own personal and professional growth, become prime candidates for dropout or burnout, and, worst of all, shortchange the very people we have been sent to serve.

Although it is implicit in the previous point, we must also establish overall diocesan policies or guidelines that specify who or which church entity finances these educational and formational opportunities. Historically, a substantial, if not the entire, portion of funding of the education and formation of our priests, deacons, and religious has come from the diocese or religious communities. Frequently, lay people have had to fund their own education or have received some modest subsidy or assistance from the parish or other church entity where they serve.

If we are serious about collaborative ministry, therefore, we must be equally serious about assisting the laity to meet the expenses associated with their education and formation. We must also look at patterns and policies for funding the ongoing education and formation of those already serving in ministry. This is a complex task that will require a new way of thinking as well as the development of new fiscal resources.

The second strategic priority that must be established if the vision of collaborative ministry is to become a reality is that of *greater linkage between the programs and services offered by our diocesan offices and departments and the felt needs within our parish communities*. The diocese is merely the sum of its parishes, and diocesan offices and departments exist to serve parishes, not vice versa. It is in the parish that the Eucharist is celebrated, that people are prepared for the sacraments, that faith formation is offered, that human needs are served, and that Christian community is experienced.

Sometimes, however, a gap can develop between the needs perceived at the diocesan level and the needs experienced at the parochial level. Several years ago, Bishop Albert Ottenweller of Steubenville, Ohio, addressed this issue at a meeting of our National Conference of Catholic Bishops. He suggested that people at the parish level often feel that they are at the bottom of a huge funnel. Everyone in the church — the pope, cardinals, national Catholic offices in Washington, the chancery, diocesan agencies — pours favorite projects, programs, suggestions, or directives into the parish funnel.

Indeed, Bishop Ottenweller's image was so compelling that it prompted one pastor to write his bishop as follows: "Reverse the funnel relationship. Find out what kind of assistance and programs we need rather than using us as objects of your pet programs."

Chapter 4

Practical Implications of Collaborative Ministry

L ET ME NOW try to draw out some practical implications of this vision of parish-based collaborative ministry for the different categories of ministers within our church.

Priests

There is probably no group within the church today more critical to implementing these strategies for pastoral planning than our ordained priests. The Second Vatican Council makes it abundantly clear that the role of the priest is unique and indispensable in the life of the church.

Paradoxically, however, the council, which speaks so positively about the priest's ministry, has also created a certain ambiguity about the role of the priest. For example, the council addressed itself extensively to the role of the bishop and the laity but offered few new insights about the role of priests.

In other words, while the council said some fine things about the priesthood, its *Decree on the Ministry and Life of Priests* was definitely among the minor ones, and the council did not develop a contemporary theology of priesthood. In fact, the council fathers seemed to take the priesthood somewhat for granted and did not see the necessity to discuss the matter at great length.

Indirectly and unwittingly the council fathers may have severely undermined the traditional role priests have played in the church. By insisting that the bishop is the primary minister in the church and that the priest is the helper of the bishop, the council demoted the priest from an *alter Christus* (another Christ) to an *alter episcopus* (another bishop). And by emphasizing the priesthood of the laity and deemphasizing the sacred power that sets the priest apart from the laity, the council deprived the priest of his traditional identity and clear self-image.

In hindsight, as Father Edward Hussey suggested in a conference on "U.S. Catholic seminaries and their future" (and it is only in hindsight), the recent decline in the number of priests and the present straits to which we are reduced are the natural and, perhaps, even inevitable result of the documents of the Second Vatican Council. What is needed today, then, is a more fully developed theology of the priesthood in light of the Second Vatican Council's emphasis on the church as the entire Christian community, on the priesthood of all the baptized, and on the pastoral ministry of bishops.

As that more fully developed theology of

the priesthood emerges, priests are faced with the critical task of contributing from their practical pastoral experience to the development of that theology and, at the same time, of being leaders in fostering a collaborative model of ministry in the church.

This, I realize is not an easy challenge. Deep down in their hearts, I suspect, many priests are haunted by the question, "Am I important?" If, for example, deacons, religious, and laity can exercise roles like those of spiritual director, leaders of scripture study groups, liturgical planners, or pastoral administrators, areas previously the priest's exclusive domain, is it any wonder that the priest's identity may be blurred and his confidence shaken?

Yet, despite the personal and ministerial ambiguity that priests may experience and the natural defensiveness such can engender, priests must be in the forefront of facilitating the development of new ministries in the church, especially on the part of the laity and, in particular, on the part of women. They must seek to learn and to exercise skills of coordination, collaboration, and community building; and they must search for creative ways to try to attract, give power to, and support others in their various ministries on behalf of God's people.

Priests, therefore, must shed those roles and responsibilities that are not appropriate for the presbyter, for example, those of business manager, administrator, maintenance man. They must not insist on doing all the preparation for baptism and marriage, on being the sole ministers of service to the youth, elderly, sick, and poor. And they must refocus on those roles that properly belong to themselves: teaching, preaching, leading in prayer and worship, and empowering or enabling deacons, religious, and laity to do what is theirs by virtue of baptism and their particular skills and training.

In this latter regard, bishops must look to priests especially to help them in the critical task of preparing people for the changes in parish life that must take place in light of the current and projected critical shortage of priests and religious. Our dwindling numbers necessitate that dioceses develop, in the immediate future, different parish configurations and staffing patterns. The priest's leadership is critical to the acceptance of what must occur.

If they deny the problem, if they become defensive because their own particular pastoral position may be threatened, or if they have not helped their people realize the rich ministerial potential they have and can develop, then people will not be ready for the transition that must happen and consequently will suffer needless trauma.

If, on the other hand, priests approach this challenge in a positive and constructive manner, and if they are able to assist their people to see the current crisis not so much as a problem but as an opportunity, an opportunity for collaborative ministry, then I am convinced we can develop new models and approaches to parish life and ministry that can be exciting, enriching, and future-oriented.

My own experience in Albany with mergers and consolidations demonstrates the critical role priests play in restructuring. In one parish, for example, which was staffed by a religious community, at the outset of the process we asked the provincial to transfer the pastor because we felt that his understanding of church and his resistance to change would be an obstacle. Unfortunately, for reasons beyond the provincial's control, the pastor was not changed and the process was an unmitigated disaster. It resulted in two years of picketing, protesting, and billboard campaigns and a year-long appeal that went to the Congregation for the Clergy and finally to the Apostolic Signatura. While the diocese was ultimately upheld, the hurt and pain inflicted was irreparable and from 75 to 150 parishioners moved into schism.

The whole experience underscored for me how critical constructive pastoral leadership

In Loving Memory of
Marino C. Curi

*Born
to Life*
February
26
1944

*Born into
Eternal Life*
February
1
2003

Safely Home
I am safely home, dear ones;
Oh, so happy and so bright!
There is perfect joy and beauty
In this everlasting light.
All the pain and grief is over,
Every restless tossing passed;
I am now at peace forever,
Safely home in heaven at last.
And He came Himself to meet me
In that way so hard to tread;
And with Jesus' arm to lean on,
Could I have one doubt or dread?
Then you must not grieve so sorely,
For I love you dearly still;
Try to look beyond earth's shadows,
Pray to trust our Father's Will.

Proko Funeral Home

is for any planning process and how any pastor can pretty much undermine the process.

If there is a silver lining in the tragedy, it's that other parishioners involved in mergers and consolidations have stated that "we're not going to embarrass ourselves and the church like the people in that particular community."

Religious

Through the living of their vowed lives of poverty, chastity, and obedience, religious offer a rich treasury of spiritual gifts for the life of the church.

As we look to the future, I envision two specific tasks religious can undertake to help develop the concept of collaborative ministry.

First, many religious have been in the vanguard of fashioning collaborative models of ministry within their own communities. They have developed creative patterns of participatory governance that rely less upon authoritarian dictates or majority rule and have fashioned patterns of effective communication that allow maximum grassroots input and facilitate sharing, understanding, ownership, and empowerment. They have also developed personnel placement policies that have allowed their members to explore more fully their particular gifts, talents, and charisms.

All of those experiences, both positive and negative, are a rich legacy from which the entire church can benefit in our pursuit of collaborative ministry. Religious, therefore, need to share their communal experience of governance, communication, and placement with the entire church so that we can reap the ripe harvest made possible by the seeds of renewal they have sown.

Second, religious need to share with the wider church the varied prayer experiences, which are so much a part of their religious life. It is frequently stated that the crisis of our age is a crisis of spirituality. We have lost a sense of the transcendent. We have lost

the art of contemplation. We have failed in
our attempts to integrate liturgy and work,
prayer and service, faith and action.

To be sure, we are struggling to move
away from that monastic approach to spirituality, which has been so dominant in our
church over the centuries. We are trying to
develop an authentically apostolic spirituality, a spirituality that enables us to harmonize
our prayer and our work, to be doers who
contemplate. We are trying to develop a spirituality that enables us to reflect upon the
wonders of the Father's creation, the beauty
of the redeemer's love, and the pulsating presence of the Holy Spirit, and then to translate
that prayerful reflection into words and deeds
that speak clearly, meaningfully, and persua-
sively to contemporary realities.

The challenge for spirituality today, in
other words, is to avoid the heresies of ac-
tivism on the one hand and escapism on the
other. And religious are in a unique position
to help us address that challenge. They have
had the experience of integrating daily prayer

with the hectic demands of their apostolates in education, health care, social work, and pastoral ministry.

This blending of the active with the contemplative in a meaningful daily pattern of prayer, which is at the heart of religious life, is something the whole church needs to experience. Indeed, prayer must be the foundation and sustaining motivation of collaborative ministry.

Religious, then, can render a real service to God's people by sharing with the whole church their time-tested and time-proven apostolic approach to prayer and by helping the members of the church to develop a style and pattern of prayer applicable to our diverse circumstances.

Deacons

As we move to make the vision of a universally ministering church a reality in our dioceses, I would suggest that deacons have several distinctive contributions to make.

First, they must be careful that they do not foster a new clericalism wherein they transfer from the ranks of lay parishioners to clerical professionals, seeking to carve out roles that solidify their own position, responsibility, and authority in the hierarchy of the church at the expense of lay initiatives and lay involvement. If that happens, the diaconate will be robbed of its fresh character and promise and will belie the concept of collaborative ministry that is so crucial for the future of our church.

Deacons, then, must see empowering the laity as one of their prime responsibilities. For example, in their function as staff members, they should seek to ensure that, whenever possible, the role of the laity is included in liturgies, programs, and activities; and they should be advocates for the laity when the laity are unable to speak for themselves. Otherwise, the deacon's efforts can be very self-serving and as discriminatory toward the laity as some clergy and religious have been and still tend to be.

Second, deacons must seek to be sensitive to the growing pains clergy and religious may experience in coming to grips with our expanded concept of ministry. Priests and religious may resent the intrusion of both deacons and laity in those roles that traditionally and historically have been reserved exclusively to them. In light of these new opportunities, it may seem that their role in the church is blurred and that their ministry has been downgraded or has lost some of its luster.

Deacons, because of their unique relationship with the clergy and religious on the one hand and with the laity on the other, can help bridge this gap by enabling priests and religious to see these new ministerial opportunities for laity not as competition, not as an usurpation of their power, and not as a threat to their authority, but as an opportunity to explore how all the gifts and ministries God has shared with people interrelate and as occasions to facilitate their development.

Specifically, deacons might discuss with priests and religious ways in which they or the laity might free them from some of the responsibilities which are not essential to their specific ministry, but with which they have become burdened. In that way, their time for prayer, study, planning, and direct pastoral ministry can be maximized.

Furthermore, deacons can discuss with the laity the reluctance they often manifest in assuming new roles in the parish or in the Christian community because "that's not my place"; and they can interpret for the laity and help them appreciate the true sense of the call, power, and responsibility they have as baptized Christians so that the laity's gifts might be fully galvanized and utilized.

Laity

The laity must come to appreciate the mission that is given to each member of the church by virtue of baptism and by virtue of one's participation in the liturgy and sacramental life of the church. While this concept of shared responsibility we described earlier is not a new or revolutionary one from a scriptural or theological point of view, historically and practically it is one that needs to be relearned and experienced.

With the Second Vatican Council and some of the movements that preceded it and flowed from it, we are just emerging from a long period in church history in which the responsibility for the mission of the church was projected to be primarily that of the clergy and religious, with little or no lay involvement, at least in leadership roles. The clergy and religious, in other words, have been perceived as exercising the main responsibility for the life, work, and mission of the church, and the role of the laity has consistently been relegated to pitching in or to helping out on a temporary standby basis when father, sister, or brother needed assistance in fulfilling that responsibility which was basically and essentially theirs.

In this understanding of church, it seemed that ordination or religious profession elevated a person to a status of spiritual superiority, to a higher state of life, to be a kind of "spiritual supermen" and "superwomen," while the laity were to plod along as best they could, but in no way were they expected to compete with the clergy and religious in theology, spirituality, or prayerfulness. However, with the people of God concept so well articulated by the Second Vatican Council, we have come to appreciate more fully that if the Gospel of Jesus is to be taken seriously at all, then it must be taken seriously by all. Thus, the council pointed out that the responsibility for the life and mission of the church is a responsibility whose dimensions are universal, applying to clergy, religious, and laity alike. All are bound together by a variety of gifts and ministries and all are called to serve the one mission, the mission of Jesus, to be served by a multiplicity of ministries and ministers.

This dignity and responsibility that each member of the Christian community has for fulfilling the mission of Jesus cannot be stressed strongly enough because unless the laity especially appreciate both the opportunity and responsibility they have to be the church, to use their gifts, talents, and energies for the building of their family and their parish community, and unless the clergy and religious foster these opportunities and encourage the fulfillment of these responsibilities, then the mission of Jesus and the mission of the parish community cannot be accomplished at all or cannot be accomplished as fully as God would have it.

What is needed more, then, is not only participation and involvement on the part of the laity in the life of the parish, but a participation and involvement that flow from an inner awareness of one's dignity as a baptized Christian and from a firm conviction about the indispensable importance of what one is doing. For example, the lector at Mass must believe firmly that he or she is reading God's word, and this word, when read with clarity, meaning, and sincerity, can touch people's hearts and give them new hope, new courage, and new direction.

The members of the parish council must believe the seriousness of the task at hand. Not only are they called to raise funds or to ratify the proposals of the parish staff, but they are also called to be concerned in earnest about the mission of the whole parish. Their participation on the council not only helps the pastor but more importantly it is a way of accepting Christ's call to them and to the community of which they are part.

The man teaching the tenth-grade confirmation class and the woman preparing second-graders for First Eucharist are not just filling in because there is a shortage of more qualified teachers. For while they might receive help from professional teachers, the pastor, or others, they themselves must appreciate and feel confident in the fact that they have the right and the responsibility to share their faith and to share their beliefs in this way.

So too must the music ministers, the special ministers of the Eucharist, the ministers of hospitality, the couples who participate in the parish's marriage preparation program, the members of the human concerns committee or the youth ministry group. The opportunities for contributing are innumerable. And each contribution made, each gift shared, each moment spent is a real participation in and extension of the mission of Jesus.

It is only when this is fully understood that the tensions and conflicts that inevitably arise in any parish, as in any family, can be put into perspective and resolved. It is only when this is fully understood that priorities can be set and plans can be made. And it is only when this occurs that one's membership in the parish can be transformed from a rather dull, routine, perfunctory fulfillment of a burdensome task or obligation to an exciting, challenging, and spirit-filled adventure that deepens one's relationship with the Lord God and redounds in loving and selfless service to God's people.

Furthermore, as the laity look to how they might collaborate with bishops, priests, deacons, and religious in fulfilling their priestly call to be collaborative ministers, I would suggest that they consider how we bishops organized the ministerial section of *Called and Gifted,* our 1980 pastoral reflection on the American Catholic laity.

After stating that baptism and confirmation empower all believers to share in some form of ministry, we go on to speak first about the laity's call to ministry in the world. It is not until after the laity's normative secular ministry is affirmed that we bishops speak about the call of laity to ecclesial or church ministry. Here the ministries of catechist, parish and diocesan councillor, eucharistic minister, and spiritual director as well as that of full-time professional minister are acknowledged with gratitude. What

Called and Gifted offers, then, is an inclusive view of lay ministry. The laity's church service is ministry, but so also is their everyday life and work, and preeminently so.

Indeed, in Bishop Raymond Lucker's address to the National Conference of Catholic Bishops at Collegeville in June 1986, entitled "Linking Church and World," he pointed out that we have reversed the order. We have tended to call the laity first to ministries within the church and then secondarily, or at least with far less emphasis, to ministries for the transformation of society.

It is important, therefore, that the laity take responsibility for correcting this imbalance. Not that they should downplay or ignore in any way the creative new church or ecclesial ministries that have been available to them in recent years. These have been vitally enriching for the whole church and must continue to flourish and expand. However, the laity must give equal attention to developing their ministries to the world, in the marketplace, in the areas of work, families, and leisure, and in all the ministries for the transformation of society.

It is especially in the family and society, in marriage and work, in human sexuality, and in economics that this transformation takes place. Consequently, it is vitally important that lay men and women appreciate the call they have in the home, on the job, and in the neighborhood or community to be about the transformation of society: to make the message of the Gospel real in the family, in social life, in business transactions, and in the world of politics.

Furthermore, the laity must strive to make the connection between faith and work, between weekend liturgy and weekday responsibilities, between seeing God's presence at the altar and at the desk, at the sink, on the farm, in the labor union hall, at the P.T.A. meeting, in the political caucus and the legislative chamber.

In the past, in other words, the church encouraged or seemed to have encouraged lay people to find holiness by leaving the world instead of finding holiness in the world. Now the laity must take the initiative to recapture and to develop practical ways to implement that sterling insight of the council that their unique role as laity is to make Christ present in society and to transform political, economic, and social institutions in light of the Gospel.

Chapter 5

Challenges

A COLLABORATIVE MODEL of parish ministry leads to practical challenges in the following four areas: (1) evangelization, (2) authority, (3) stewardship, and (4) Sunday worship.

Zeal for Evangelization

There was not a parish I visited or forum I conducted in my four-year parish visitation program that people did not raise the concern of evangelization: of reaching out to the 17 million Catholics who are alienated from their faith or to the 90 million of our fellow

Americans who are unchurched. Yet with all the concern about evangelization there seems to be little follow-through.

To me, it's not so much a lack of programs or resources that is at the root of the difficulty but the need to foster in parishioners the inner confidence to share their faith with others in an informal, noncoercive, and nonjudgmental manner.

For despite the clear mandate we as Christians have to share the message and mission of Jesus with others, there are many obstacles to fulfilling this command, two of which are particularly noteworthy in the contemporary milieu.

The first is the *growing secularization* of our age that has eroded a sense of the spiritual in our lives. For far too many, human life today is lived without reference to the transcendent, to that which lies beyond what we can see, hear, taste, touch, and smell. This, then, translates into a rather mechanistic or functional approach to life that cannot deal with questions of ultimate meaning. Possessions, power, and pleasure easily become our dominant societal values, and a competitive model of human relations becomes the way to achieve them. In this model, the self becomes the center of the universe; other people are things to serve one's needs; efficiency is the moral norm; whatever works is the means, let the chips fall where they may — be these the chips of unethical business practices, abortion, adultery, euthanasia, or whatever else suits one's convenience.

The secularization of our age then dampens both our energy and enthusiasm to evangelize as well as the receptivity of those with whom we would share the Gospel message.

A second impediment to our motivation for evangelization is a *cultural phenomenon*. With all the emphasis that our society places on choice, pluralism, and individuality, the idea of proselytizing, that is, of sharing the good news with those who have never heard the message or with fellow Catholics or Christians who have been alienated from the church or have become indifferent to the practice of their faith, may seem arrogant or at least insensitive on our part. In other words, we have become uncomfortable in sharing our Catholic values, beliefs, and traditions with others because we are afraid these will be offensive to them or because we are afraid that we may seem judgmental or condescending, failing to respect their religious choices, decisions, or convictions. And so many, bowing to these social and cultural niceties of our day, have lost the energy, zeal, and enthusiasm necessary for evangelization. At least I know this has been a problem for myself personally, and I don't think I am unique in this regard.

For example, before becoming bishop of the diocese of Albany, I worked in the inner city. During that period I had no problem at all in responding to people's emotional or physical needs, no problem at all talking to all kinds of groups about the theological imperative of social ministry, no problem at all delivering homilies, celebrating the Eucharist and the sacraments. However, when it came to speaking with another person on a one-to-one basis about the Christian life, especially if that person did not initiate the conversation, I literally froze, feeling that this would be unprofessional or coercive, or feeling just plain awkward and uncomfortable in the situation. On the one hand I rationalized that I was trying to avoid the pitfall of rice Christianity, namely, the pitfall of offering people assistance on the condition that they accept our faith. However, in my heart of hearts, I realized that I was allowing my self-image and my fear of human respect to get in the way of my baptismal commitment and ordination responsibility to preach the good news of our Lord Jesus Christ both in season and out of season.

Or to take another example, a few years ago I attended a workshop on evangelization. One of the exercises at the workshop was to pick out someone else in the room, someone whom you did not know personally, and share with that person who Jesus is for you. Although everyone in the room was a committed Catholic, most of them clergy, and although the sharing took place on a one-to-one basis, not in front of the entire group, I found it very difficult to share my faith in this way.

This awkwardness in sharing our faith or prayer experience is why the Catholic community has such difficulty coping with the growing trend toward fundamentalism within our society and why our efforts at evangelization at times have been so impoverished. It is also why our response to Pope John Paul II's call for a new evangelization is so urgent and critically important.

Tensions Regarding Authority

As the laity, deacons, and religious assume more roles and responsibility in the life of the church, it seems to me there is a need for appropriate and consistent nomenclature across the diocese and across the country for the ministries that are being exercised. Otherwise tensions and misunderstanding will inevitably arise. The bishops committee on the laity is currently doing a comprehensive study of this issue. This will obviously necessitate the need for criteria for ministry, job descriptions, just wage scales, and mechanisms for accountability.

As the parish reorganization study points out so well, there is also the tension that arises from how authority is exercised in the church and how collaborative decision-making and accountability are lived out in practice.

The tension arises from two very important theological principles that coexist in our Vatican II church. On the one hand, the Second Vatican Council emphasizes the common dignity and equality that exists among all the members of God's priestly people. All, therefore, are called to the same holiness of life, and all are entitled to become actively engaged in exercising the church's mission to the world. On the other hand, the council also highlights the hierarchical nature of the church. We live as believers within a church that has an appointed structure with predetermined ranks of authority.

These two notions so evident in the documents of the council and of the revised code of canon law are not contradictory, but they do create a tension when it comes to such practical things as how decisions are made in the church. This tension is real at the level of the universal church, and it also affects our local church or diocese and our parish communities.

We are faced with the challenge of living with this tension, with these two differing notions. One side stresses our unity with Christ Jesus and with one another; the other side stresses the need for organization, structure, and authority. One side acknowledges the gifts of God that exist within individual believers; the other side stresses the diversity of functions and roles that must be lived out within the Christian community. Somewhere between them we are expected to govern and

to be governed, to minister and to be minis-
tered to. The challenge, then, is to recognize
the authority of those who hold pastoral office within the church without diminishing
the value of those who recognize their call to
shared leadership responsibility arising from
baptism, confirmation, and the Eucharist.

More specifically, the pastor, by church
law, has ultimate responsibility for the spiritual care of the parish. He is directly
accountable to the diocesan bishop for all
parish matters.

However, it is neither wise nor based upon
sound church teaching if the pastor operates
without consultation with others.

That is why canon 536 of the revised code
of canon law encourages the establishment
of parish councils. It is interesting to note
that the code calls this body a pastoral council. The idea behind the term used contains a
subtle hint: pastoral parish councils ought to
be dealing with comprehensive pastoral ministry in the parish and not just finances or
temporalities.

The pastoral or parish council, however, according to the code, is of a consultative or advisory nature. But do not let these terms diminish or dilute the important and indeed indispensable role of the council. The real purpose of any consultative or advisory body is the pooling of the gifts of the group to influence the decisions to be made. The decision itself may lie ultimately with another (e.g., the pastor or dean or vicar or bishop), but the real controlling element is the group's influencing the decision by doing their homework and by sharing their combined wisdom. In this way the persons consulted in many respects determine what the decision will be.

In very pragmatic terms, then, the pastor continues to bear the final responsibility for the total parish ministry. For the sake of accountability to the diocesan bishop whom he represents and to the people of God whom he serves, the pastor must ratify the recommendations of the parish council before they can be implemented. Likewise the pastor must guard against the parish council's endorsing proposals that would be contrary to universal church law, diocesan policy, or civil law.

On the other hand, the pastor is expected to exercise his pastoral responsibility not as the only minister of the parish, but as the presider over the variety of ministries that the people have and as a sharer with the people in those ministries. Rarely, therefore, would it be envisioned that the pastor override or veto the advice of the parish council, and if such be the case, then normally an explanation of his decision would be in order. Hopefully, too, the advice given the pastor from the council would not be by majority rule but by consensus among the group.

In the final analysis, councils will work better once pastor, staff, and council members realize that there will probably always be some creative tension between the executive function and the wisdom or advisory function. Each has its own vantage point and needs to be understood in that light. The more, however, pastor and council members clarify their mutual expectations of each other and the way decision-making is formulated, the better off our planning efforts will be. And what I have said of the relationship between pastor and parish councils can also be said about the relationship between the bishop and the diocesan planning office with regard to whatever processes and structures are established to develop plans for parish restructuring.

Stewardship as a Way of Life

A study by Bishop William McManus and Father Andrew Greeley entitled *Catholic Contributions: Sociology and Policy* reveals that although American Catholics earn on the average over $1,000 a year more than their Protestant counterparts, Catholic financial contributions to their church are much less than those of Protestants. For example, on the average, Protestants contribute $580 to their church annually as opposed to $320 for Catholics. Furthermore, Catholics contribute only 1.1 percent of their income to the church, while Protestants donate at the level of 2.2 percent of their income.

More strikingly, the study finds that the disparity between Catholic and Protestant giving is the result of a dramatic change in patterns of contributions to one's church over the past twenty-five years. In the early 1960s, Catholics gave the same proportion of their income to the church as Protestants. In the last quarter century, however, the Protestant giving rate has remained stable at approximately 2 percent of annual income while the Catholic rate has fallen from more than 2 percent to about 1 percent.

Why has this occurred? Is it that Catholics have become stingier or more miserly? I hardly think so. Is it due to the changing levels in church attendance? No, because Protestant church attendance has declined significantly more than Catholic in this time frame, but their level of giving has not. Is it because Catholics give to their schools rather than the church? Statistics reveal that this is not the case because parents who send their children to Catholic schools contribute more rather than less to the church than do other Catholics.

I believe that the decline in the pattern of Catholic giving to the church is due primarily to a lack of communication and a lack of leadership.

From experience, I am convinced that when our people know the need and understand the case, they are always most generous. Information, fact sharing, and accountability on the part of church leaders are critically important for reversing the declining trend of giving to our church. But something more is needed, namely, the insights and motivation that will enable our Catholic people to see the connection between their donations and their faith and worship. That nexus is the concept of stewardship, which is more than just an approach to fund raising but rather a way of life. It is a practical and tangible response to the call to be God's people and to exercise collaborative ministry in the church.

For many Catholics, stewardship is an unfamiliar word, but it is an idea that is biblically rooted. Quite simply it is a commitment in faith that responds to the scriptural call to work with and through each other to build the kingdom of God here on earth. It involves the three t's — the giving and sharing of one's time, talents, and treasure in service to the Lord and to our brothers and sisters in need in the community about us.

Stewardship, in other words, is an authentic Christian lifestyle. It is not something we leave at the door on Sunday morning and pick up the following week. Rather it is something we live every day. It is a deep commitment to the person of Jesus Christ and to his call to discipleship. If we maintain that Jesus is our Lord and that we have committed our life to him, then we should do what he asks us. And what he asks his followers is to become involved and to share of themselves totally, not only of what they possess financially but, equally important, of their time and of the special gifts or talents they have received from God.

Stewardship, then, is not about money; it is about faith. Money is involved but only as an expression of faith, only as a way to translate one's relationship with the Lord, nurtured by prayer and the sacraments of the church, into concrete action.

Sunday Worship

Fourth, and finally, but certainly not least important let me address the issue of Sunday worship in the absence of a priest. The parish restructuring study found that the primary concern of parish reorganization efforts is to maintain the nature and identity of the church as a eucharistic community.

> In words attributed to Augustine, "The church makes the Eucharist, the Eucharist makes the church." This "chicken-egg" reciprocal rela-

tionship between church and Eucharist appears circular: to make Eucharist, you have to have church. On the other hand, the celebration of the Eucharist is essential in making church. Given (*a*) the theological relationship among community leadership, eucharistic presidency, and sacramental ordination, (*b*) the dwindling number of priests, and (*c*) the relationship between Eucharist-making and church-making, it is not surprising to find a common, even overarching concern in parish reorganization efforts for preserving the eucharistic identity of parishes. On a practical level, dioceses approach this matter in a variety of ways, depending on where they enter the "church-Eucharist" circle. Some seek to preserve vibrant parish communities that are capable of a life-giving celebration of the Eucharist even if they must compromise on the frequency with which that celebration occurs. Others seek to reconfigure parish communities to ensure, as much as possible, the weekly celebration of the Eucharist. Even those who raise questions about the prudence and long-term effect of Sunday worship in the absence of a priest as well as those who call for a reexamination of who can preside at the Eucharist are affirming the essential nature of the church as a eucharistic community. (*Diocesan Efforts at Parish Reorganization* [Conference for Pastoral Planning and Council Development, 1995], 81)

On a personal note I believe that we should not develop plans for our parishes or clusters that include "Priestless Sundays." I realize that often on weekdays, communion services are already being conducted when a priest is away or unavailable. This I applaud. Also, in the case of an emergency, when a priest wakes up sick on a Sunday morning, people should be trained and prepared to conduct a communion service for the congregation.

However, in planning regular weekend liturgies when the priest may be unavailable because of vacation or a sabbatical, adjustments should be made that would insure a full Eucharist at each liturgy, even if this may mean reducing the number of Masses or encouraging people to attend Eucharist at a neighboring parish.

The Eucharist is at the heart of our Catholic Christian heritage. It is at Eucharist that the church comes together as church. It is at Eucharist that we are reminded of who we are and what it is we are called to be. It is at Eucharist that we are energized to change our wants, our wills, our loves, and our desires. Therefore, the people have the right to a full Eucharist each weekend, and when this does not occur, I fear in the long run we may lose our Catholic Christian identity.

Indeed, in some places throughout the country where weekly Eucharist is impossible and communion services are conducted on a regular basis, people have begun to miss the distinction between such services and a full Eucharist. They frequently refer to "Father's Mass" or "Sister's Mass" or "the Deacon's Mass." Given the pastoral realities in most dioceses, I believe that we can develop schedules that insure the opportunity for a full Eucharist each Sunday.

Conclusion

Every generation in the church faces its own unique challenges. We today are faced with the task of birthing the vision of collaborative ministry that the Second Vatican Council articulated. We do so in a time of great social upheaval when the forces of secularization are making inroads and eclipsing the Christian vision of life that has prevailed in Western civilization for centuries.

In the face of this challenge and the tension and pain it produces, some have become discouraged and disillusioned. They experience only the confusion and turmoil borne of renewal and change. When age-old moorings have been cut and we are set adrift, they conclude that the situation is hopeless or impossible.

Quite frankly, I do not share this bleak outlook. I am convinced that we are living in one of the greatest periods of renaissance in the long history of Christianity. There are certain times in the life of the world and our church when the Holy Spirit is poured forth abundantly, creating a new vision and a new horizon that give shape and direction to humankind and civilization for generations to come.

We are living in precisely such an age, in a new Pentecost. And we have a golden opportunity to become involved at the heart of this reawakening, of being forerunners of the church of tomorrow, of being molders and builders of a new theological language and new ecclesial structures that speak to our contemporary society and that insure a fresh hearing for the Christian message. It will take all of the zeal, talent, maturity, vision, and love we possess if we are to respond to this call as God desires and as the challenge itself so urgently demands.

As we stand on the threshold of the new millennium, then, I hope that we all can accept, embrace, and fulfill this challenge for the honor and glory of God, for the sanctification of our brothers and sisters in the community around us, and for the transformation of the world and society in which we live.

ALSO BY

HOWARD J. HUBBARD

I AM BREAD BROKEN
A Spirituality for the Catechist

"Each ministry in the Church demands its own
reservoir of spiritual depths. Bishop Hubbard shows
how the catechist can plumb that well and become
a saint in the process of doing so."
— *Rembert G. Weakland, O.S.B.*

Reading *I Am Bread Broken* is like being with a wise
and discerning spiritual guide, one who understands
well the pathways of the soul, and one who values the
intellectual life. Catechists will find here support and
challenge for their high calling, as will other
ministers, ordained and lay."
— *Dolores R. Leckey*

0-8245-1575-7; $9.95 (paper)

Please support your local bookstore, or call 1-800-395-0690.
For a free catalog, please write us at
THE CROSSROAD PUBLISHING COMPANY
370 LEXINGTON AVENUE
NEW YORK, NY 10017

We hope you enjoyed Fulfilling the Vision.
Thank you for reading it.

crossroad
herder